BROADSTAIRS
AND
ST PETER'S
IN OLD PHOTOGRAPHS

POLICEMEN OF THE SKIES OVER BROADSTAIRS

POLICEMEN OF THE SKIES OVER BROADSTAIRS, 1939, an aerial view taken from a Manston RAF Avro Anson aeroplane. (*ITG*, 13 May 1939)

BROADSTAIRS
AND
ST PETER'S
IN OLD PHOTOGRAPHS

COLLECTED BY
JOHN WHYMAN

ALAN SUTTON

Alan Sutton Publishing Limited
Phoenix Mill · Far Thrupp · Stroud · Gloucestershire

First Published 1990

British Library Cataloguing in Publication Data

Broadstairs and St Peter's in old photographs.
1. Kent. Broadstairs, history
I. Whyman. John
942.2357

ISBN 0–86299–523–X

This book is dedicated to the efforts of past chairmen, members and officers of the old Broadstairs and St Peter's Urban District Council who did so much to promote the reputation and well-being of the locality and its residents.

Front Cover Illustration:

BLEAK HOUSE FROM BROADSTAIRS PIER, 1952, showing the well-known public house, the Tartar Frigate, the pier look-out and storehouse, the back of the sands of Viking Bay and in the background Bleak House, for which Broadstairs is internationally famous. This picture sums up for many people what Broadstairs is all about. (Margate Museum).

Typeset in 9/10 Korinna.
Typesetting and origination by
Alan Sutton Publishing Limited.
Printed in Great Britain by
Dotesios Printers Limited.

CONTENTS

AERIAL VIEW, 1953, showing the pier and harbour, the Main (Viking) Bay, the Victoria Gardens and Clock Tower and further inland where there are still open and unbuilt areas. (Margate Museum)

INTRODUCTION

For eighty years prior to the establishment of the Thanet District Council in 1974, Broadstairs and St Peter's had functioned as an Urban District Council (UDC), having previously been administered by a Local Board from 1879 to 1894. Over many centuries a parochial cohesion had existed between these two old and distinct settlements, St Peter's being the senior parish, and the original core of the whole locality, with a fine Norman church dating from 1070. Holy Trinity church in Broadstairs, by contrast, was erected between 1828 and 1830, with an ecclesiastical parish for the town being formed out of St Peter's on 27 September 1850.

The two parishes taken together still contain some agricultural land, a variety of residential and commercial development and a cliff coastline encompassing several bays, beginning at the Margate end with Botany Bay, followed by Kingsgate and Joss Bays, across the north Foreland, famous for its lighthouse to Stone Bay, the Main Bay at Broadstairs, renamed Viking Bay in 1949, running into Louisa Bay and finishing up with Dumpton Bay, nearest to Ramsgate. These features, along with the formerly detached settlements of Kingsgate and Reading Street, are all referred to in this volume.

VICTORIA PARADE, C. 1871, from what was then the Assembly Rooms and is now the Charles Dickens public house, formerly Anderson's café, looking towards Dickens House and the Albion Hotel. (UKC Library)

Prior to the middle of the eighteenth century, the local economy was dependent upon activities associated with the land and the sea. St Peter's was a farming community and Broadstairs and Kingsgate were maritime communities. Broadstairs possessed a harbour and a wooden pier and its inhabitants lived from fishing (including sharing in the Icelandic cod fishery), boat-building (associated with the White family) and repairing, legitimate coastal trading, along with some smuggling, and foying, which included going out to vessels in distress. A new dimension was introduced by sea bathing and the expansion of holidaymaking, the first bathing machine being introduced to Broadstairs in 1754.

The combined population of Broadstairs and St Peter's was still small at the beginning of the nineteenth century, with only 1,568 people enumerated when the first official census was taken in 1801. The two settlements remained distinct as they had been in the eighteenth century and before. Their merging over time was due to the more rapid growth of Broadstairs as a seaside resort. The tendency, however, for Broadstairs to outstrip St Peter's both in terms of numbers and settlement density was a long drawn-out process. Even as late as 1841, within a combined population of 2,978, St Peter's still had sixty more inhabitants than did Broadstairs. Thereafter it was Broadstairs which forged ahead.

THE HIGH STREET in the 1950s, showing The Viking restaurant and, further on, an advertisement for Kodak Films. (Margate Museum)

There have been many famous visitors to the seaside resort of Broadstairs, including the widowed Duchess of Kent and her daughter, Princess, later Queen, Victoria, who resided in Pierremont House for part of the summer of 1829; and Charles Dickens between 1837 and 1851. He wrote affectionately in 1851 of 'Our Watering Place' in his already popular Victorian weekly journal, *Household Words*. There can be no doubt that Dickens brought fame to Broadstairs, building on its well-established reputation as a select, family resort. These characteristics have been preserved to the present day, Broadstairs being contrasted to Margate and Ramsgate as follows, as early as 1799: 'those who may not chuse to mix in the gaiety and pleasure of a more public place, will find this a retired and agreeable situation'. Much later, in the early 1900s, someone observed that, 'Broadstairs has not developed into a second-rate Margate or a third-class Ramsgate!' The memory of Charles Dickens lives on in his associations with Bleak House, Dickens House, the Albion Hotel and other buildings, but above all in the Broadstairs Branch of the Dickens Fellowship and the Dickens Festival, inspired by Miss Gladys Waterer, which has been held annually since 1937, excluding the war years.

Despite strong and well-documented Dickensian associations, Broadstairs is

THE PADDLING POOL between Louisa Bay and the Main Bay, below the Clock Tower, in the late 1940s. (Margate Museum)

not to be thought of as primarily a Victorian town. Indeed, its architectural features tend to be either Hanoverian, Edwardian or very much post-Edwardian. By 1871 the combined population of Broadstairs and St Peter's was still under 4,000, well short of what Margate's population had been in 1801. Expansion has occurred over the past one hundred years, however, incorporating additional hotels, boarding-houses and apartments, schools, convalescent and retirement homes, and an explosion of residential housing, raising the combined population to 10,095 by 1911, compared to 5,661 in 1891.

The pace of expansion has been particularly pronounced since the 1930s. The 1950s and the 1960s witnessed the peak of residential holidaymaking, under the stimulus of guaranteed paid holidays, continually rising living standards and the motor car. As against an Urban District Council population of 12,748 in 1931, 15,081 were recorded for 1951, rising to 18,920 by 1971. Since the 1970s domestic holidaymaking has been considerably undermined by the increasing popularity of foreign holidays. Present-day Broadstairs retains a residential appeal and is a haven for the retired. It also attracts numerous day visitors and foreign students attending summer language schools. Sadly, Mr Edward Heath's annual

BOWKETT'S CAKES BAKERY, Westwood, Wednesday 21 April 1937, the date of the opening of Mr A.H. Bowkett's new bakery on the Ramsgate Road, with its electric clock. (*ITG*, 24 April 1937)

carol concert is a thing of the past, but since 1965 Broadstairs has acquired an international reputation for its annual folk festival. The population of Broadstairs and St Peter's today exceeds 23,000.

This book seeks to present an animated and living record of the area through the eyes of photographers. The emphasis is on people and events rather than on scenes and buildings, the latter being lavishly portrayed in guidebooks and on postcards. The book draws wholly on photographic evidence which has been selected from three principal sources: firstly, from a few early photographs in the library of the University of Kent (UKC Library); secondly, from the published photographs and preserved negatives of two local newspapers, The *Isle of Thanet Gazette (ITG)* and The *Thanet Times (TT)*, from the 1920s on; and, thirdly, from the negatives and photographs, also dating from the 1920s and after, which were produced by the Sunbeam Photo Company of Margate, and are now the property of Margate Museum. There are several advantages attaching to newspaper photographs. Almost invariably they concentrate on specific people and events which were being reported when the photographs were taken. There is the likelihood that many of them have been forgotten or, at least, not been seen for some time. Perhaps their greatest merit arises, however, from precision in dating.

The approach adopted by this book, ranging from the aerial photograph to the very specific event, is both topographical and thematic. It has not been thought necessary to provide a separate introduction to each section. Instead, the captions speak for themselves. Indeed, a caption speaks for each individual photograph, the source of which is immediately acknowledged in brackets, as indicated above.

Broadstairs before 1914

ELDON PLACE, C. 1871, showing also Eagle House or the House-on-the-Sands. Here, under the cliff, there was formerly a shipbuilding yard. In 1926 this site was acquired by the Broadstairs and St Peter's UDC, following which the Garden-on-the-Sands Pavilion was erected as a place of entertainment in 1933. (UKC Library)

HORSE-DRAWN BATHING MACHINES, c. 1871, standing at the harbour end of the Main Bay in front of the bathing rooms, with Eldon Place on top of the cliff, Harbour Street, York Gate and Holy Trinity church tower in the background. Note the steps down to the bathing machines and the towels or bathing costumes drying at the rear of the bathing house. Bathing machines were introduced to Broadstairs in 1754. (UKC Library)

BATHING MACHINES, Nos 3 and 5, c. 1871. Note the 'modesty hood' at the back which was lowered to guarantee privacy while bathing or descending the rear steps, a refinement dating back to before 1753 and attributable to a Margate Quaker, Benjamin Beale. Note to the left on the cliff top the abrupt termination of the Victorian building line. (UKC Library)

'MODEST LITTLE BROADSTAIRS' VIEWED FROM THE CLIFFS, 1895, from a photograph by Frith & Co. Broadstairs was then described as 'quieter and more select than its larger and noisier neighbours, and . . . especially in high favour with family parties, who find quite a little paradise on the sheltered beach.' The one bathing tent is well outnumbered by the bathing machines at the water's edge. (*Round the Coast*, published by George Newnes Limited)

VICTORIA GARDENS in the 1890s, overlooking the Main Bay, prior to the extension of Bleak House in 1901. The Victoria Gardens were opened by Princess Louise in 1892. Note the horse-drawn bathing machines at the water's edge, a collier at anchor in the harbour, and the *Marie Forbes-Barton* lifeboat which was then stationed on the pier. (Dr J. Whyman)

EDWARDIAN BATHING MACHINES LINED UP IN THE MAIN BAY. They belonged to Mr Oliver William Marsh, who is seen standing alone on the fourth machine from the right. During the 1900s he owned forty-eight machines. (*TT*, 19 December 1967)

TAKING THE SUN, C. 1914, outside the look-out and storehouse, better known today as the boat-house, on Broadstairs pier. Sitting to the right of Bill 'Sugar' Bishop (standing) is Teddy 'Porky' Croom, father of Jack Croom, followed by either Arch or Jack Hiller. (*ITG*, 26 January 1968)

SECTION TWO

Central Broadstairs

LOOKING UP THE HIGH STREET in the 1950s: Bowkett's cake shop, O. Robinson & Sons, Ltd, builders, the Arts and Crafts Jewellers, the Prince Albert public house, the entrance to the Bohemia Theatre and, almost out of sight, a Shell garage. (Margate Museum)

LOOKING DOWN THE HIGH STREET in the 1950s, with Lloyds Bank on the left and Barclays Bank at the bottom. Also shown are the Prince Albert public house, D.M. Wickham, the fruiterers, next door to David Greig, the grocers. Redman's, gentlemen's outfitters and tailors, established in 1863, occupied the corner site with Belvedere Road, pointing the way to the Methodist church and to Martin Walter's garage and advertising the estate agents Cockett, Henderson & Co., greyhound racing at Dumpton Park and local cinema performances. (Margate Museum)

DEMOLITION OF TWO FLINT SHOPS, 1957, believed to be over 300 years old, at the junction of the High Street and Belvedere Road, in order to solve a traffic bottle-neck in the town's main shopping centre. Prior to demolition the buildings belonged to Redman's, the outfitters (as seen in the previous photograph), and J.E. Swann, a confectioner. Plans to widen the High Street at this point in 1914 had come to nothing because of the First World War. (*ITG*, 15 March 1957).

COSTUMED DICKENSIANS WALKING DOWN THE HIGH STREET, June 1968, from Pierremont Park to the sea front during the anual Dickens Festival. On the extreme left is the late Miss Vautier and to her left, wearing a top hat, is Mr J.B. Read, then chairman of the local branch of the Dickens Fellowship. On the extreme right is Miss Joyce Smith, the current chairman, walking alongsdie the late Mrs Pam Towe. (*ITG*, 21 June 1968)

FATHER CHRISTMAS, 1956, being conveyed down the High Street on an improvised sleigh, fitted with wheels, to open a Christmas bazaar at the 4th Broadstairs Scout headquarters on Saturday 8 December. (*ITG*, 14 December 1956)

BROADSTAIRS WAR MEMORIAL AND FLORAL OFFERINGS, June 1923, shortly after its unveiling and dedication in a commanding position at the entrance to Pierremont Park by the Archdeacon of Canterbury, the Ven. L.J. White-Thomson, a former vicar of St Peter's. (*ITG*, 16 June 1923)

THE WAR MEMORIAL BEING CLEANED on Sunday 15 October 1961 by fifteen members of the Broadstairs Round Table, under their chairman, Mr Bill Bryan. (*ITG*, 20 October 1961)

REMEMBRANCE SUNDAY, 12 November 1961, Cllr F.E.J. Amies, the chairman of the Broadstairs and St Peter's UDC, laying his wreath on the town's war memorial. Observing from the background are Mr Ted Robinson, Cllr L. Rigelsford, the Revd W.C. Watkins of Christ Church (Free Church of England) in Osborne Road, some girl guides, and, on the extreme right, Miss J. Reeves. The two clergymen to the right of Cllr Amies are the vicar of St Peter's, the Revd T. Prichard, wearing the white surplice, and the minister of the Vale Congregational church, the Revd A. Lister-Hetherington. (*ITG*, 17 November 1961)

A FINAL TRIBUTE TO SIR WINSTON CHURCHILL from the Broadstairs and St Peter's UDC on Saturday 30 January 1965, when its chairman, Cllr E.V.L. Neville, laid a wreath of white carnations, blue iris and red tulips at the town's war memorial. Standing to attention in the background are Cllr Norma Booth, Cllr L. Rigelsford and, on the extreme right, the clerk of the UDC, Mr H.C. Norris. (*ITG*, 5 February 1965)

PIERREMONT HALL, 1963. The official opening of the Broadstairs Dickens Festival by the chairman of the Broadstairs and St Peter's UDC, Cllr E.E. Bing, was only the second time that the chairman of the council had opened the annual festival week. (*TT*, 18 June 1963)

THE ANNUAL FOLK FESTIVAL in Pierremont Park in the late 1960s, giving visitors to Broadstairs the opportunity of exhibiting their dancing skills. The festival celebrated its twenty-fifth anniversary during August 1990. (Margate Museum)

4TH BROADSTAIRS SCOUT TROOP, July 1955, digging the foundations for their new hut at Belvedere Road. Mr L. Read, secretary of the troop's Parents' and Friends' Committee, is on the extreme left and the scoutmaster, Mr S. Lacey, is on the right. (*ITG*, 8 July 1955).

BRADSTOW HOUSE, HIGH STREET, BROADSTAIRS, August 1924, the branch office for the *Isle of Thanet Gazette* and the *Thanet Times* and also the publishing office of the *Broadstairs and St Peter's Gazette*. (*ITG*, 9 August 1924)

CHINESE LANTERN CAFÉ, in Albion Street, 1 June 1927 the scene of a local murder. (*ITG*, 4 June 1927)

MRS SONIA RAMSAY, the 1927 murder victim, who, as a 'well-known lady' and the café's proprietress, was discovered dead in a bedroom 'with a terrible wound on her forehead'. (*ITG*, 4 June 1927)

LOOKING THROUGH YORK GATE in the late 1920s towards the sea and an advertisement for 'Broadstairs Pure Rock' at five prices from 1d. to 1s. What had originally been the bathing rooms now served refreshments and C. Harrison, at 23 Harbour Street, was a fishing-tackle dealer. York Gate, an arched portal, originally defended by a portcullis and strong gates, and erected by George Culmer in 1540 as a protection against privateers, was repaired in 1795 by Sir John Henniker Bt. On the extreme left, 22a Harbour Street was the premises of a ladies' hairdresser, Elisé Williams, who had worked in London's West End, hence the partly obliterated sign for permanent waving, etc. (Margate Museum)

CHARLES DICKENS'S MEMORIAL TABLET ON BLEAK HOUSE, facing the sea, as photographed in 1953. Undoubtedly the most frequent literary visitor to the Thanet coast, Charles Dickens (1812–70) spent twelve holidays in Broadstairs between 1837 and 1851, and in 1850 he rented Fort House, later renamed Bleak House. At an auction held at the Royal Albion Hotel during October 1952 there were no bidders for Bleak House at a reserve price of £8,000. (Margate Museum)

BLEAK HOUSE, Thursday 16 June 1955, 'the perfect setting' for the Dickensian tea party which was a new feature of the year's Dickens Festival. Sitting on the left is Mrs Myrtle Nuthall. (*ITG*, 17 June 1955)

A NEW OWNER FOR BLEAK HOUSE, Mr Charles Eade sitting in Charles Dickens's study in 1959, chatting to Broadstairs councillors, from right to left, E.V.L. Neville, L. Rigelsford and E. Valsler. (*ITG*, 12 June 1959)

Pier, Harbour and the Main (or Viking) Bay

BROADSTAIRS PIER, c. 1947, with an artist at work. Pier is Thanet nomenclature for what would otherwise be referred to as a jetty or quay. Broadstairs pier dates back to the sixteenth century, its original shape and position being similar to what we see today. Fronting the hatted gentleman is a raft from the Cunard liner, the *Lusitania*, sunk in the Atlantic by a German submarine in May 1915 with the loss of over 1,000 lives. To the right of the raft is one of the five safety boats which were unnamed but numbered, this one being No. 2. Note also the series of wooden steps from the sea to the pier, the pier crane, the booking kiosk for Uncle Mack's Minstrels, whose evening performances took place in the shelter, the wooden roof of which had a canvas extension during the summer months. The vessel leaving the harbour is the *Topsy*, belonging to Cllr H. Bing. It was high tide on a slightly misty day when this photograph was taken. (Margate Museum)

RELAXING ON THE PIER, late 1940s, with Cosy Nook, Bleak House and the cliffs to the north of Broadstairs extending to Stone Bay and the North Foreland. Apart from under the gardens of Cosy Nook, the cliffs were unprotected in those days and on neither side of the Main Bay were there any promenades beneath the cliffs. (Margate Museum)

THE HUGGETT FAMILY OF BBC FAME, Sunday 27 June 1954, at the end of Broadstairs pier. Joe Huggett (Jack Warner) is fishing, and Ethel (Kathleen Harrison) is watching from a deckchair. With them are their two 'children', Jane (Vera Day) and Bobby (Anthony Green). (*ITG*, 2 July 1954)

HERRINGS BEING LANDED from boats in the harbour, in October 1965. Shown here are some of the traditional wherries associated with herring fishing which, during the summer months, ran boat trips for local residents and visitors. From left to right can be seen the *Perseverance*, the *Spray*, *La Mouette*, *Uncle George*, the *Irex* and, finally, the *Ruby*. Wearing the woolly hat on the extreme left is George Strevens and facing him in the centre is Jack Croom. (*ITG*, 29 October 1965)

NORTH GODWIN LIGHTSHIP, Wednesday 29 December 1937. Gifts which had been taken from Broadstairs in the motor boat *Perseverance* are presented on board by Mr E.A. Anderson and friends. The senior master, Captain W. Hover, is in the centre. Behind him on the right are 'Mopper' Sherred, and Shah Hiller, wearing the cheese-cutter or peaked cap. (*ITG*, 1 January 1938)

FISHERMEN MENDING THEIR NETS ON THE PIER, late 1940s. From left to right are shown Shah Hiller, Jimmy Foreman, Bill 'Sugar' Bishop, 'Dinky' James and Arch Hiller. Note on the extreme right a UDC notice relating to the *Lusitania* raft. (Margate Museum)

BROADSTAIRS BOATMEN, Jack Croom (on the left) and Bill Taylor, taking advantage of a fine, sunny day to get on with painting one of their boats, the *Spray*. (*ITG*, 19 February 1965)

BROADSTAIRS HARBOUR, autumn 1968, taken by the *Isle of Thanet Gazette* cameraman, Frank Howe, 'Kent's Photographer of the Year'. Twenty-five years later he is still the newspaper's chief photographer. Attending to the nets is Bill Holness, who started his working life as a smack apprentice and served on fishing trawlers throughout the Second World War. (*ITG*, 18 October 1968)

ART EXHIBITION on Broadstairs pier, 1953, the pictures being for sale and teas being advertised. (Margate Museum)

'THANET GALE HAVOC', 31 January 1953. The great storm that winter literally pounded Broadstairs pier. (*ITG*, 6 February 1953)

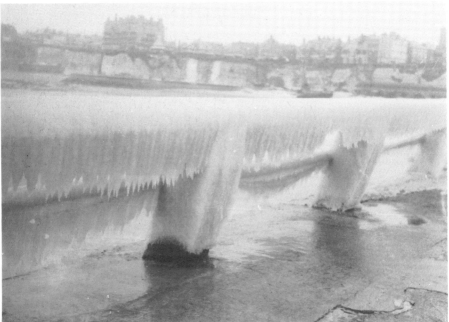

AN ICY SCENE on Sunday 20 January 1963, when waves crashing over Broadstairs pier formed a fantastic twelve-inch thick barricade of ice along the outer railings. (*TT*, 22 January 1963)

NIGHT-TIME REPAIRS TO THE PIER. On the night of Monday 13 November 1961 it was a cold, tough job for these council workmen, 'working against the clock with a quick-drying cement to block a hole caused when coping stones were dislodged by [a] gale'. Supervising them in a raincoat was the UDC road foreman, the late Mr Fred Page. (*ITG*, 17 November 1961)

PREPARING THE SLIPWAY for the 1968 season. Mr Fred Carter-Nock is seen coating quicklime to clear marine growth, wearing goggles, an air-filter and protective clothing which was bright green. (*ITG*, 24 May 1968)

A NEW SAFETY BOAT, the *Stella Maris*, launched by the Rt Hon. Mr Edward Heath on Sunday 4 May 1969 before a crowd of local residents and holidaymakers. Mr Heath is seen standing on the pier steps alongside the chairman of the Broadstairs and St Peter's UDC, Cllr L. Rigelsford. Cllr E.E. Bing is seen speaking through a microphone. Aboard the safety boat are James Warburton, the chief safety boatman, on the left, and his assistant, Terry Day. Among those observing from the pier are Mrs Rigelsford, Cllr Bertie White, and Mr W.R. Rees-Davies, MP, the hatted gentleman being Mr W.G. Heath, Edward Heath's father. (*TT*, 6 May 1969)

VISIT OF THE MINESWEEPER HMS *RATTLESNAKE* on Thursday 21 July 1955. Accompanying a demonstration in Viking Bay, Lt.-Com. R. Garner, the commanding officer, is greeted by the chairman of the Broadstairs and St Peter's UDC, Cllr H.E. Seccombe, as he steps ashore. To his left is Mrs Seccombe, and facing her on the extreme left is Mr Arthur Pay in his uniform as harbourmaster. On the extreme right is Cllr E.V. Neville. (*ITG*, 22 July 1955)

'SEA EMPTYING IN PROGRESS', Saturday 2 July 1966. As part of their rag day, Dane Court School pupils are attempting to empty the sea at Broadstairs harbour. (*TT*, 5 July 1966)

THAMES TELEVISION FILMING, ON BROADSTAIRS PIER on Monday 23 February 1970, members of the Broadstairs Dickens Fellowship turned out in costume for a documentary on the life of Charles Dickens. Actor Michael Jayston played the part of Dickens and Sheila Grant his wife. 'The Old Tea Shop' is advertised in the background. From right to left, starting with the second lady, are Miss Joyce Smith, Mrs Lillian Taylor, Mrs G. Semper, the late Mrs Pam Towe and Mrs Betty Trull. (*ITG*, 27 February 1970)

LAUNCHING THE *KENT*, the 1st St Peter's Sea Scouts' new vessel, at Viking Bay, on Monday 19 April 1965. Mrs M. Burgoyne, with speech in hand, is shown performing this pleasant duty. Immediately behind her from right to left are the vicar of St Peter's, Canon T. Prichard, Com. Burgoyne, former officer with HMS *Kent*, and Dr David Chastell. Facing Mrs Burgoyne is the Scout leader of the troop, Bill Taylor. The vessel being launched had been built in Ramsgate at a cost of £500, having been specially designed for the Sea Scouts. (*ITG*, 23 April 1965)

A YOUNG ARTIST and children on the beach in the 1940s. Note the crane on the pierhead. (Margate Museum)

ABOARD THE *DAISY WHERRY* in the harbour, *c*. 1950, in the capable hands of Jesse Hiller. The boat moored on the left against the first set of wooden steps belonged to the then owner of Bleak House, Mr Albert Batchelor, of Blue Circle Cement. He was one of the first to own a private aeroplane, which he piloted himself into Manston aerodrome on weekend visits to Broadstairs. (Margate Museum)

SETTING OFF IN THE *PERSEVERANCE* in the 1950s, with Jack Croom at the tiller and Frank Croom at the engine. The dark-coated gentleman at the front is Mr L. Kent. Note in the background the (red) wing floats, the first boating concession for holiday makers allowed in Viking Bay. (Margate Museum)

AN OIL-POLLUTED BEACH, 5 May 1967, where a bulldozer is at work clearing the oil pollution on Viking Bay. (*TT*, 9 May 1967)

OIL FROM THE BEACH being shown to Cllr E.E. Bing, chairman of the UDC Entertainments, Pier and Harbour Committee, by the harbourmaster, Mr Jim Bowyer. (*TT*, 9 May 1967)

THE GARDEN-ON-THE-SANDS in the later 1940s, showing the 'Pram Park' in the foreground and the Pavilion beyond. (Margate Museum)

PRAMS ON THE MAIN BEACH, 1952. Note Eagle House or the House-on-the-Sands, and the main steps leading up to the Promenade and Victoria Parade. (Margate Museum)

THE MAIN BAY, C. 1930, looking in the opposite direction from the previous picture, showing a variety of tents, a refreshment kiosk offering teas and ices and further along, Uncle Mack's Minstrels' stage on the beach. Anderson's café and the Albion Hotel are visible on top of the cliff. (Margate Museum)

UNCLE MACK'S MINSTRELS in the early 1930s. The posters advise people to book their seats for evening shows on the pier at 8.00 p.m. Note in front of the UDC deck-chairs a free enclosure for children sitting on the sands. (Mrs V.G. Whyman)

BROADSTAIRS' NEW BATHING STATION

SKETCH PLAN OF THE NEW FERRO-CONCRETE BATHING STATION, sanctioned in January 1935 by the Broadstairs and St Peter's UDC for the Main Bay, to include sixty-six bathing cubicles and thirty-two chalets, the roof forming an 'undercliff promenade'. (*ITG*, 26 January 1935)

THE BATHING STATION in the 1930s, below Anderson's café, the Victoria café and, on the extreme left, Morelli's Ice Cream Parlour. Note the safety rowing boat, numbered '2', at the ready in the Main Bay. (Margate Museum)

THREE WOMEN AND A DOG on deck-chairs on the main beach in 1921. (Postcard photograph, Dr J. Whyman)

'AUGUST? NO, EASTER MONDAY!' April 1955, on Viking Bay, 'where visitors lazed and sailed in . . . brilliant weather'. (*ITG*, 15 April 1955)

THE FRENCH TRAWLER, *JEAN PIERRE ET PHILLIPE*, on Sunday 11 November 1962, embedded in the sand of Viking Bay after having run aground at Broadstairs. (*ITG*, 16 November 1962)

ICE FLOES ON THE SEA, during the Arctic winter of 1963, with the wreck of the *Jean Pierre et Phillipe* in the foreground. (*TT*, 1 February 1963)

CELEBRATING GUY FAWKES, 5 November 1968, with a large bonfire at Viking Bay. (*ITG*, 8 November 1968)

SEA-WALL DEFENCES UNDER CONSTRUCTION, 1962. Watched by August holidaymakers, workmen toil below high-water mark on the second stage of the UDC's three-part programme of costly sea defences. This second stage, costing £75,000, covered the coastline from Preacher's Knoll to Louisa Bay. (*ITG*, 17 August 1962)

SHRIMPING IN VIKING BAY in the 1950s. (Margate Museum)

'MR BROADSTAIRS' (Mr Frank Douglas, well known as an artist, writer and repertory actor) with children on the beach in 1949. Note the appropriately decorated bucket. For the 1950 season he was re-engaged for the main ten weeks 'to delight his many young friends with fun and games and all kinds of surprises'. (Margate Museum and the *Broadstairs Guide* of 1950)

DONKEY RIDES AT VIKING BAY, 1953. From right to left the first two headbands read 'Ray' and 'Tommy Steele'. Note in the background the lift up to the Albion Hotel, the Omar café and Marchesi Bros restaurant. (Margate Museum)

'SMOKEY' THE CLOWN (Mr Townsend), in July 1958, entertaining children on the beach with his accordion. (*ITG*, 1 August 1958)

BEACH SPORTS, 1953, involving a girls' race. Note the stage for Gerald Stafford's Punch and Judy show. He and his wife are standing on either side of it. (Margate Museum)

AN ADULTS' WHEELBARROW RACE, 1953. The notice on the extreme left informs the public that 'An area will be roped in when the tide is out for CHILDREN'S COMPETITIONS'. Next to it is the stage for Gerald Stafford's Punch and Judy show, immediately behind Mrs Stafford. Note the diving boards which were placed every summer at the end of the pier. (Margate Museum)

ENJOYING PUNCH AND JUDY ON THE BEACH, 1953. The next show for children and adults is at 11 o'clock, price 3d. each. Cecil Barker is the main attraction at the Pavilion. (Margate Museum)

PUNCH AND JUDY, July 1955, being enjoyed by a 'large crowd of youngsters – and a few grown-ups'. Note, in the background, a first-aid station and the beach kiosk selling 'Eldorado' ice cream. (*ITG*, 22 July 1955)

VIKING BAY *DAILY MAIL* SAND-CASTLE COMPETITION in the 1950s, the participating children wearing Red Indian head-dress. Also advertised is *Le Figaro*, as joint sponsors of the competition. (Margate Museum)

SUNDAY PICTORIAL BEACH BEAUTY CONTEST in the 1950s, asking 'Are you the VENUS of Broadstairs?' or 'Are you the MARILYN of Broadstairs?' (Margate Museum)

THE PETER PAN EXPRESS, mid-1960s, Viking Bay, the nearest locomotive carrying the number 1748. (Margate Museum)

LEAVING THE BEACH, C. 1960, via the passenger lift at 4d. for adults and 2d. for children under twelve. Season tickets, at 5s. weekly and 25s. for the whole season, are advertised and the public is invited to ring for the lift. (Margate Museum)

The Promenade, to Victoria Parade and Gardens, and the Clock Tower

EMERGING FROM THE LIFT, c. 1960, on the Promenade in front of Marchesi's restaurant and the Omar café. Advertised as 'NOW RUNNING' and ideal for invalid chairs and prams, no one could fail to notice its location with three arrows pointing to the entrance. Electrically driven, it is now more than eighty years old. (Margate Museum)

ALBION STEPS, near the lift, on Saturday 3 July 1965, where a small boy is offering his mite, helping to start a pile of pennies grow in support of the Cancer Relief Fund. Observing closely on the extreme right is Cllr J. Epps. (*ITG*, 9 July 1965)

THE OLD BROADSTAIRS STAGE-COACH on the Promenade with members of the local branch of the Dickens Fellowship during the 1956 Dickens Festival. During the 1880s this coach operated from the Albion Hotel to Canterbury and Dover. The second lady from the left is Mrs Pitts. Mrs Wilson Smith is holding a doll, standing next to Mrs P. Owens in black. On board the stage-coach are Mr Edward Berry, facing the ladies and wearing a grey top hat, and, in front, Mr Bill Mason, wearing a black top hat. Between them are children from the American USAF base at Manston, the boys wearing bow-ties. (*ITG*, 22 June 1956)

CARLTON LODGE, VICTORIA PARADE, formerly the Carlton Hotel, 1955, a London County Council seaside home for retired people, offering accommodation to fifty-one men and women. In this picture, taken on Wednesday 20 July 1955, the chairman of Broadstairs and St Peter's UDC, Cllr H.E. Seccombe, and his wife (on his right) meet some of the residents. On his left is the matron, Mrs Deer. (*ITG*, 22 July 1955)

KENTISH MORRIS DANCERS performing on Whit Monday 1962 on the Promenade before a crowd of spectators, with Morelli's Ice Cream Parlour in the background. (*ITG*, 15 June 1962)

VICTORIA GARDENS in the 1930s, showing an open top tramcar and looking along Victoria Parade. Tram services were discontinued in March 1937. Note the bandstand on the Promenade. (Margate Museum)

THE VICTORIA PARADE END OF VICTORIA GARDENS in the 1930s, showing just in front of the Carlton Hotel an open-top tramcar advertising Mackesons. Further along is the Wilmot Hotel, the sign for which is obscured by a tree. (Margate Museum)

PLAQUE COMMEMORATING UNCLE MACK (Mr J.H. Summerson), who had entertained Broadstairs residents and visitors for over fifty years from 1895 to 1948 with his minstrel troupe. This memorial was placed on the Promenade opposite Victoria Parade following his death in 1949, at the age of seventy-three. It was paid for by public subscription. (Margate Museum)

THE PLAQUE BEING DEDICATED in 1950, before numerous happy onlookers, by Miss Annette Mills, famous for *Muffin the Mule*, and sister of Sir John Mills, the actor. She is seen standing alongside the chairman of the Broadstairs and St Peter's UDC, Cllr Frederick B. Salt. (Margate Museum)

STROLLING ALONG THE PROMENADE in the 1920s. Note the parasols, the deck-chair ticket collector in front of the hedge and, to his right, uniformed schoolboys. (Margate Museum)

PROMENADE STROLLING in the 1920s, showing part of Chandos Square, the spire of the York Street Methodist church and Victoria Parade, stretching along to Anderson's café and Dickens House, on a fine summer's day. Those occupying the deck-chairs to the right have a grandstand view of Uncle Mack's performance on the Main Beach. (Margate Museum)

LOOKING DOWN ON THE MAIN BAY, in the early 1930s, thought it is partly obscured by plants and vegetation. Prominent is Eagle House, or the House-on-the-Sands, with teas, etc. being advertised on the roof of the café at the bottom of Harbour Street. This picture was taken prior to the construction of the Garden-on-the-Sands Pavilion in 1933. (Mrs V.G. Whyman)

BANDSTAND AND CLOCK TOWER, overlooking the paddling pool, in the late 1940s. The time is 4 p.m., the performance having commenced at 2.45. The bandstand is decorated and illuminated at night and there is no shortage of parked cars on Victoria Parade. Note, too, the early loudspeakers around the bandstand. (Margate Museum)

VICTORIA GARDENS in the 1960s, just before midday according to the Clock Tower. (Margate Museum)

WESTERN ESPLANADE, in the late 1940s, with children on horses and ponies. (Margate Museum)

SECTION FIVE

Louisa and the Outer Bays

LOUISA BAY in 1952, where children take donkey rides against the background of a crowded beach and the Grand Hotel. (Margate Museum)

THE GRAND HOTEL in the 1930s above a very crowded Louisa Bay where public bathing tents are for hire, though to the extreme right people are changing on the beach. (Margate Museum)

THE *CORBIERE* ON THE ROCKS NEAR LOUISA GAP, 1930. After being delayed seventeen days in the English Channel due to rough weather, this French fifty-ton motor ketch was driven aground in a strong north-easterly gale at about midnight on Saturday 15 February 1930, following which the crew were hauled up the eighty-foot cliffs by means of ropes. (*ITG*, 22 February 1930)

A WRECKED SALOON CAR near Dumpton Gap in March 1958. A Mark 1 Cortina, having been pushed over the cliff, a drop of sixty to seventy feet, now nestles in a cove. Note how the cliff had collapsed, frost possibly having destabilized the cliff face. (*ITG*, 28 March 1958)

DUMPTON BAY, c. 1950, with bathing station and tents, deck-chairs for hire and a beach kiosk. The surrounding area was still predominantly agricultural. (Margate Museum)

DUMPTON BAY, c. 1930, looking towards Broadstairs, offering bathing tents and a kiosk advertising pure ices, teas and refreshments. (Margate Museum)

DUMPTON BAY in 1946 showing some early protective support for the cliffs near the public shelter on the Western Esplanade. (Margate Museum)

COASTAL PROTECTION WORK, well in hand by January 1961, between Dumpton Gap and Louisa Bay, as 'the first stage of a major development to carry the work farther around the cliffs, as far as Preacher's Knoll, Viking Bay, [consisting of] a concrete sea-wall protected by an inclined concrete apron and pre-cast blocks in the form of steps to break the waves', at a cost of £39,800. (*ITG*, 20 January 1961)

BEACH CHALETS IN LOUISA BAY in the 1960s. The promenade was the result of sea-wall defences carried out in 1962. (Margate Museum)

STEPS TO STONE BAY from the Eastern Esplanade in the late 1940s. (Margate Museum)

STONE GAP in the 1930s, the North Foreland entrance to Stone Bay, a track compared to the steps of today. (Margate Museum)

THE OLD ST MARY'S HOME FOR CHILDREN, May 1958, which had stood as a notable landmark between Stone Road and the Eastern Esplanade, was demolished by Mr F.B. Salt, who was planning a residential development for the site. (*ITG*, 23 May 1958)

COASTAL PROTECTION, February 1970. Commencement of the work from Broadstairs harbour to Stone Gap, the cost to Broadstairs ratepayers after government and county council grants being estimated at £40,000 out of a total cost of £350,000. (*ITG*, 27 February 1970)

STONE BAY, July 1970, and work in progress on the coastal protection project. Note the recent residential development along the Eastern Esplanade. (*ITG*, 24 July 1970)

DRAMA ON THE NORTH FORELAND. On Wednesday 24 August 1955 Napoleon Green, a twenty-two-year-old airman stationed at the Manston USAF base went berserk, killed three servicemen and battled with police on the beach near the North Foreland in full view of holidaymakers before turning his rifle against himself. Here on the Cliff Promenade four policemen, USAF personnel and a county ambulance await developments. (*ITG*, 26 August 1955)

NORTH FORELAND RADIO STATION, Rumfields, on Tuesday 3 November 1959. Mr A. Ogilvy, the officer in charge, is showing visitors the switchboards, to mark the fiftieth anniversary of the Post Office marine radio communication service. On his left is the chairman of the Broadstairs and St Peter's UDC, Cllr E.F. Owen. Behind him to the right is Cllr E.E. Bing. (*ITG*, 6 November 1959)

NORTH FORELAND in the 1950s. An aerial view of the second most easterly point in England, showing very clearly the lighthouse which has been a tourist attraction since the eighteenth century. Over the last thirty years there has been much residential infilling. (Margate Museum)

JOSS BAY in the 1930s, revealing stacked deck-chairs, beach tents and chalets, with a covered terrace to the beach café advertising Walls ice cream, teas and minerals by Ozonic. Standing at the water's edge are the safety-boat wheels. (Margate Museum)

JOSS BAY late August 1957. Mid-week meanness by a number of visiting motorists is indicated by a long line of cars parked at right angles to the cliff stretching along Elmwood Avenue – free! Farmhands are at work near a notice warning motorists of a concealed entrance to the beach. Beyond the cars is the North Foreland golf course. (*ITG*, 30 August 1957)

JOSS BAY, same date. The UDC car park above the bay is half-empty! (*ITG*, 30 August 1957)

JOSS BAY, as it appeared on that summer day in 1957 – a truly crowded and popular beach, windshields having made their appearance. (*ITG*, 30 August 1957)

JOSS BAY over the crowded Whitsun holiday period in 1962. Cars are parked not only along Elmwood Avenue, but also on the pavement, despite a 'No Waiting' police notice, since the official cliff-top car park is filled to capacity. (*ITG*, 15 June 1962)

JOSS BAY, on Tuesday 9 June 1960, when seventeen children and five mothers from Limehouse took part in a television programme in the series *Pursuit of Happiness*, accompanied by its interviewer, Daniel Farson. The outing included a picnic and a Punch and Judy show. (*ITG*, 10 June 1960)

JOSS BAY, in January 1966, after gales had driven the sand up to the level of the cliff top. (*TT*, 18 January 1966)

GIANT GRAIN ELEVATOR, KINGSGATE, September 1946. When Thanet was hit by one of the worst gales within living memory on the night of Friday 20 September 1946, this elevator being towed to Odessa by a Russian ship was swept ashore on to the rocks beneath the cliffs at Kingsgate. (*ITG*, 27 September 1946)

KINGSGATE BAY, Thursday morning, 4 April 1957. Police bring a casualty ashore, five having been lost from a crew of fourteen when the 900-ton coaster, *Lisbeth M*, collided in thick fog with the 3,700-ton collier, *Sir John Snell*, two miles off Kingsgate Bay. The *Lisbeth M* sank within half an hour, its nine survivors being rowed ashore through the fog by the lifeboat of the *Sir John Snell*. The constable with a moustache is PC Harold Goode. Note on the cliff face a warning notice advising the public not to sit under the cliffs. (*ITG*, 5 April 1957)

KINGSGATE CASTLE, August 1968. Yards and yards of tubular scaffolding mounting the cliff face under Kingsgate Castle as the first phase in the difficult task of restoring the cliff to a safe condition, the owners of the thirty-two flats there having accepted the £25,000 cost of the necessary cliff protection work. (*ITG*, 23 August 1968)

KINGSGATE CASTLE HOTEL in the late 1920s, belonging to North Foreland Hotels Ltd, whose managing director, Mr Reuben T. Peace, had purchased it in 1922 from Lady Avebury, the widow of Lord Avebury, PC, LLD, DL, JP, DCL, FRS, FSA. Distinguished as an author and scientist, he was perhaps best known for having been the patron saint of St Lubbock's Day, a reference to his associaiton with the Bank Holiday Act of 1871, which introduced the August bank holiday, when he was Sir John Lubbock, MP. Note at the door the liveried member of staff and guests relaxing on the lawn. (Margate Musuem)

KINGSGATE CASTLE HOTEL FANCY DRESS BALL, 1926. This was a popular end of August event. (*ITG*, 4 September 1926)

KINGSGATE CASTLE HOTEL, 1934, showing the Gothic tapestries in the newly decorated drawing room. Other 1934 improvements included central heating and a hot water system. (*ITG*, 14 April 1934)

THE CAPTAIN DIGBY, 1952. People enjoying respectively a few pints and a pot of tea looking out over Kingsgate Bay and Castle. (Margate Museum)

BEACH CHALETS AT KINGSGATE BAY, 1960s, with bathing costumes and towels hanging up to dry in the background. The gentleman reclining across two chairs, exposed to the northerly breezes, is obviously trying to keep warm. (Margate Museum)

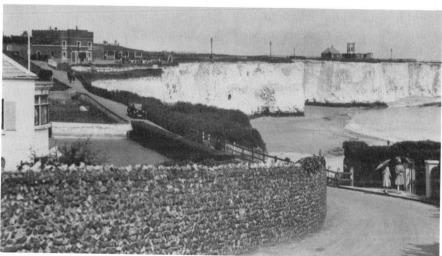

KINGSGATE BAY in the 1920s. A car travelling from the popular inn, the Captain Digby, is passing Holland House. Note how narrow the road is. Note, too, on the cliff, the Kingsgate lifeboat house, Neptune's Tower, and to its right the coastguard hut. Today only the base of the tower survives. Little Holland House is shown on the extreme left followed by Holland House and the coastguard cottages, only the front gardens of which are shown. Clearly visible, however, are the coastguard mast and in the cliff face a smugglers' cave, which could be reached from the beach and ran up to the Captain Digby. (Margate Museum)

KINGSGATE BAY, February 1959, where a section of the cliff face is being reinforced to stop erosion, the road to the Captain Digby having been closed, though wines, beers and spirits are still on sale. (*ITG*, 20 February 1959)

KINGSGATE BAY, February 1959, men reinforcing the cliff face, showing an ex-army quad four-wheel drive truck. The men are not wearing any protective clothing. (*ITG*, 20 February 1959)

BOTANY BAY in the 1920s, showing the Prince's Walk to Margate. Note the unstable cliff face, which does not deter people from sitting under the cliff. (Margate Museum)

CONVENT ROAD, running inland from Kingsgate Bay, in the 1920s. Note the Chinese paper parasols. (Margate Museum)

LANTHORNE ROAD in the 1920s. (Margate Museum)

HORSE-RIDING ON CALLIS COURT ROAD, c. 1960. (Margate Museum)

St Peter's and its Surroundings

ST PETER'S VILLAGE SIGN in the 1930s, outside the entrance to the church. Following a speech by HRH the Duke of York, later King George VI, at the Royal Academy in 1920 on the revival of village signs, the *Daily Mail* organized a village signs competition and exhibition, offering a total of £2,200 in prizes. Ten awards were made and the design from which this sign was constructed won the first prize of £1,000. (Margate Museum)

ST PETER'S WAR MEMORIAL, after being unveiled and dedicated by the Bishop of Dover on Wednesday 17 June 1925. (*ITG*, 20 June 1925)

ST PETER'S CHURCH, Sunday 24 April 1955. 'With church and flag as a symbolic background, Thanet South Scouts file in for the St George's Day parade.' (*ITG*, 29 April 1955)

ST PETER'S CHURCH, Monday 13 February 1961, showing seven of the thirty-strong bellringers' team in the belfry. From left to right are Madeline Walton, Mrs Nellie Bridges (the captain), her late husband, William Bridges, Pauline Fennell, Mary Taylor and the late Mr Wellington. (*ITG*, 17 February 1961)

ST PETER'S CHURCHYARD, October 1966, Canon T.E. Prichard, the vicar, inspecting the damage to one of the graves following the heavy rains of that month, when about a hundred graves had sunk into the ground by up to eighteen inches. (*TT*, 1 November 1966)

Above:
ST PETER'S HIGH STREET, on Sunday 27 April 1952, was the scene of a disaster long to be remembered in the annals of St Peter's. On that evening a blazing American Thunderjet dived on the High Street, demolishing a sub-branch of Lloyd's Bank and an iron-monger's shop and killing three people instantaneously; the pilot, Capt. Clifford Fogarty, and the ironmonger and his wife, seventy-nine-year-old Mr William Read and fifty-five-year-old Mrs Evelyn May Read, who were found buried deep in the cellar beneath the bank and shop. Fortunately, the street was almost empty, thanks to the vicar, the Revd L.C. Sargant, having extended his sermon by ten minutes. This picture shows all that was left of the bank, the ironmonger's shop and Mr and Mrs Read's home. (*ITG*, 2 May 1952)

Right:
ST PETER'S HIGH STREET, Sunday 27 April 1952. Willing hands help the occupiers of nearby houses to remove their posses-sions. (*ITG*, 2 May 1952)

ST PETER'S HIGH STREET, early 1960s, looking towards the church. The Cottage Tea Room, offering 'Morning Coffee & Teas' and 'Home Made Cakes', had been opened by Miss Ann Hayter and Miss Ball following the 1952 American jet crash. The blank side-wall on the extreme left denotes the spot where buildings had been demolished in the disaster. (Margate Museum)

NO. 94 RUMFIELDS ROAD on Thursday 20 November 1952, when less than three feet separated all that remained of a Tiger Moth and the back wall of the house, the aeroplane having plunged into the back garden of Mrs W. Baxter, having hit the 120 ft tall mast at the North Foreland Wireless Station. (*ITG*, 28 November 1952)

READING STREET on Saturday 14 May 1960. Members of the choir of St Andrew's church, shown in the centre of the picture, head the procession taking the Queen of the May, Barbara Sadd, aged twelve, to her coronation. She had been chosen for that year for her regular attendance at the 'Children's Church'. (*ITG*, 20 May 1960)

READING STREET, May 1963. The May Queen for 1963, Maureen Mellican, after the crowning ceremony at the village green, sits beside Prince Charming, Jacqueline Fright, with their attendants, all being members of the St Andrew's Sunday School. (*TT*, 7 May 1963)

READING STREET, 1969. Mr E. McEnery, the president of the Working Men's Club and Institute Union, cutting the first sod of earth for the new convalescent home in Reading Street, in front of the chairman of the Broadstairs and St Peter's UDC, Cllr L. Rigelsford. (*TT*, 4 March 1969)

READING STREET, October 1970. The new convalescent home overlooking the North Foreland golf course, is nearing completion, and being inspected by Mr G. Janner, the Labour MP for Leicester North-West, while staying in the family's home at Stone Road, Broadstairs. (*ITG*, 9 October 1970)

READING STREET, Thursday 28 December 1961. Detective Inspector Pearce, head of Margate and Broadstairs CID with Detective Constable Beard and senior fire officers on the burnt-out roof of the East Kent Carton Manufacturers Company factory, following its destruction by fire the previous night. (*ITG*, 29 December 1961)

READING STREET, Tuesday 25 February 1958. Mr C. Hodson stands next to his garage and workshop, which had been wrecked in a gale. (*ITG*, 28 February 1958)

READING STREET, Tuesday 17 February 1970, following a blizzard at breakfast time. (*ITG*, 20 February 1970)

READING STREET ROAD, February 1958. Detectives are investigating a sensational Broadstairs murder, following the strangulation on Thursday 6 February, of fifty-two-year-old Miss Lillian Kathleen Chubb, of 105 Hugin Avenue, St Peter's. (*ITG*, 14 February 1958)

NORTHDOWN ROAD, ST PETER'S, on Monday 1 March 1965, following the opening of the new all-metal footbridge across the railway line, which cost £5,500. (*ITG*, 5 March 1965)

HAINE ROAD on Wednesday 3 January 1968, when a heavy rainstorm caused part of the grass verge to subside. A weak patch was hit by this East Kent bus bound for Ramsgate, both inside wheels slipping off the road into an adjacent field, forcing the driver to abandon his vehicle. (*ITG*, 5 January 1968)

DANE VALLEY TIP, October 1970, with piles of rubbish deposited outside due to industrial action by council manual workers. (*ITG*, 9 October 1970)

DANE VALLEY TIP on Monday 19 October 1970, with just one week-end's accumulation of rubbish dumped outside by householders. Two days earlier Broadstairs firemen had tackled a blaze here. (*ITG*, 23 October 1970)

WESTWOOD, Thursday 5 March 1964. The chairman of the Broadstairs and St Peter's UDC, Cllr E.E. Bing, switches on the first traffic lights in Broadstairs, watched by Cllr A.T. Tucker, the chairman of the Building and Works Commitee, the surveyor, Mr Roy Plackett, and Police Inspector W. Beton. The road junction at Westwood was one of the town's blackest accident spots, with fifty-one accidents during the previous three years. (*TT*, 10 March 1964)

WESTWOOD, January 1960. Three lorries and a car bumping and bouncing their way over pot-holed ice on the Ramsgate to Margate Road, including a Bowkett's Cakes lorry. (*ITG*, 22 January 1960)

Commerce and Agriculture

BOWKETT'S CAKES BAKERY, Westwood, April 1937. The interior of the main bakery shows a block of six modern continuous brick ovens. (*ITG*, 24 April 1937)

THE MALE STAFF OF BOWKETT'S CAKES BAKERY, April 1937, with Mr Bowkett sitting in the front row and four van drivers in the back row. (*ITG*, 1 May 1937)

MR A.H. BOWKETT'S ANNUAL STAFF SUPPER AND DANCE, 1938, held at the St George's Hotel in Margate. (*ITG*, 12 March 1938)

BROADSTAIRS PUBLICITY VAN for 1960, manned by two Broadstairs hoteliers, Mr and Mrs Loveland, being visited in Pierremont Park by the chairman of the Broadstairs and St Peter's UDC, Cllr E.F. Owen. It is a Martin Walter caravan, made in Kent, hence the advertisement and an invitation to take a catalogue. Mrs I. Loveland, as a member of the Broadstairs Hotel and Boarding Association, ran the Aralia Hotel, 7 Stone Road, Broadstairs, which was AA and RAC listed, and open all the year. (*ITG*, 29 January 1960)

BROADSTAIRS PUBLICITY VAN outside Pierremont Hall, advertising the advantages of access resulting from the new Dartford-Purfleet tunnel which opened in 1963. Motorists could 'bypass London by this splendid quick route and visit Broadstairs'. This touring van served as a 'Mobile Information Centre'. (Margate Museum)

ADVERTISEMENTS, 1925, for the Broadstairs removers, Thompson & Son, 71 and 73 High Street, and Silver Queen motor-coach outings, including an all-day circular trip to Folkestone for 5s., and an afternoon circular trip to Canterbury for 3s. 6d., bookable from Bradstow House in the High Street. (*ITG*, 18 April 1925)

UPTON HOUSE, Vale Road, Broadstairs, 1965. Mr E.B. Watson with his 1926 Lagonda. (*ITG*, 5 March 1965)

DIXONS GARAGE, Belvedere Road, Broadstairs, June 1931, advertising the Austin 'Twelve-Six', 'at the astonishing price of £198'. (*ITG*, 20 June 1931)

MARTIN WALTER LTD, Belvedere Road, Broadstairs, September 1938, advertising the new Vauxhall '12 four'. (*ITG*, 10 September 1938)

THE WROTHAM ARMS, Ramsgate Road, at the corner of Wrotham Avenue, June 1926, in an advertisement featuring 'Kent's Best Inns'. (*ITG*, 26 June 1926)

ANDERSON'S CAFÉ, VICTORIA PARADE, BROADSTAIRS, June 1924, now the Charles Dickens public house, being introduced to the public. Kelly's directories list this café through to the end of the 1950s. (*ITG*, 14 June 1924)

B.J. PEARSON, AUCTIONEER AND ESTATE AGENT, STATION GATES, BROADSTAIRS, 1927 advertisement. (*Kelly's Isle of Thanet Directory and Guide for 1927*)

THANET PLACE, just off the North Foreland Road, Broadstairs, April 1955. 'Furnishings under the hammer': a member of the staff of B.J. Pearson & Son begins cataloguing the furnishings of Thanet Place, sitting under a solid silver chandelier, valued at £600, which is said to have hung in one of the palaces of the last Czar of Russia. (*ITG*, 7 April 1955)

THANET PLACE, April 1955, occupying land which once belonged to a school where for a time Sir Winston Churchill was educated. Thanet Place, as a 'fabulous Italianate residence' was built in 1927 at a cost of £200,000 for Sir Edmund Vestey, Bt., standing in spacious grounds of ten acres. Sir Edmund began with a weekly wage of 2s. 6d.; he died a millionnaire. In his day 'the beef baronet' used to sit with his binoculars watching the passing of his Blue Star Line ships to ascertain whether they were on schedule. (*ITG*, 7 April 1955)

THATCHING A RICK, 1952, with the North Foreland Lighthouse in the background. Note the farm implements which are fairly antiquated by today's standards. (Margate Museum)

ELMWOOD FARM, August 1964, where thirty acres of barley are being harvested in the shadow of the North Foreland Lighthouse. Behind the wheel is Jim Sladden, while Mrs Elizabeth Lyon, the farmer's wife, takes care of the bagging of the grain. (*TT*, 18 August 1964)

ELMWOOD FARM, August 1964. While farmer Alastair Lyon drives the tractor, Mrs Rose Wood takes care of the loading of bales. (*TT*, 18 August 1964)

ELMWOOD FARM, August 1964. Ted Foley and John Rumbold hard at work in the grain-cleaning shed. Behind them is an Ideal grain cleaner and to their right a sack marked 'Broadstairs'. (*TT*, 18 August 1964)

AN OLD PARTLY THATCHED FARM IN ST PETER'S in the 1920s, with the church in the background. (Margate Museum)

Wartime Broadstairs, 1939–45

WARTIME DESOLATION. Broadstairs High Street as it appeared during the August Bank Holiday of 1940, looking up to Raglan Place and Serene Place, with neither motor car nor human in sight. Films could be developed at the chemists, Timothy Whites & Taylors, 6 High Street, next door to the estate agents, Reeve & Bayley. The taking of pictures, however, was prohibited since the coastline during the Second World War was a restricted area. Effectively, holiday resorts ceased to function as such. When war was declared thousands of visitors went home; hotels, boarding houses, entertainments, etc. closed down; private schools moved to other parts of the country and children were evacuated. (Photographed by Mr G.W. Everest)

ST PETER'S CHURCH on Monday 6 May 1940 saw the marriage of Miss Joan Winifred Dawson, eldest daughter of Mrs Heathorn (of Bay Trees, Kingsgate Avenue, Broadstairs) and the late Mr H.C. Dawson, to Flying Officer Alex Beresford Speedy Hallsworth, only son of Mr and Mrs Hallsworth of New Zealand. (*ITG*, 10 May 1940)

PRISONERS OF WAR AT STALAG XX A, May 1942, were employed in 'delivering coal to German housewives'. This photograph was sent home by Private Stanley Norman Kemp, serving with the Buffs, son of Mr and Mrs H.L. Kemp, of 6 Astor Road, Reading Street, St Peter's. Private Kemp, an old boy of Holy Trinity School, Broadstairs, is second from the left in the back row. (*ITG*, 15 May 1942)

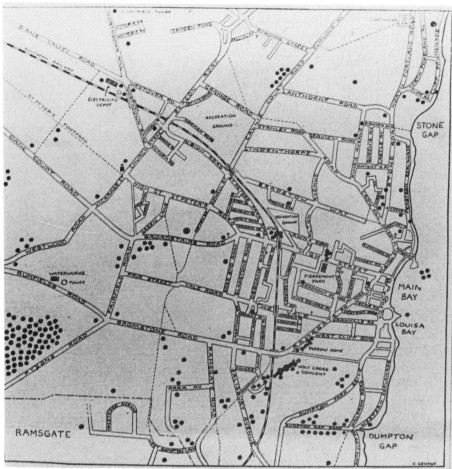

THE BOMBING OF BROADSTAIRS AND ST PETER'S up to November 1944. Since the outbreak of war Broadstairs had experienced 2,463 air-raid warnings, 86 shell warnings and 1,165 immediate alerts. Broadstairs sustained 278 high explosive bombs and over 300 incendiary and other bombs as well as the only two flying bombs experienced in Thanet. Only seven civilians, however, lost their lives, though forty-nine were injured, with seventeen buildings being destroyed or damaged beyond repair and a further 3,238 damaged but reparable. This map shows where over 200 of the 278 high explosive bombs fell. More than thirty exploded on the rocks or in the sea at Joss Bay and five exploded close together on the golf links near the Captain Digby at Kingsgate. There were 595 high-explosive bombs dropped in the borough of Margate and 692 in Ramsgate. (*ITG*, 6 October 1944 and 10 November 1944)

'PELHAMDALE', BROADSTAIRS ROAD, ST PETER'S, Monday 10 July 1944: 'Flying Bomb in Back Garden, Girl's Remarkable Escape'. The reference is to Miss Betty Hughes, daughter of Mr and Mrs Herbert Richard Hughes, there being only three slight injuries, caused by glass and debris, when in the early hours of that morning 'a flying bomb exploded and crashed into the back garden of a house in southern England'. Newspapers were forbidden to divulge the exact locations when bombs fell on to residential properties, but detective work in a Kelly's directory has revealed the above address for Mr and Mr H.R. Hughes, who were named in the press report of this incident. The picture shows the rear of their house after the bomb had exploded, the blast having completely ripped off the back of the house, exposing all four rooms. Mr and Mrs Hughes, sleeping in a front bedroom, were also unhurt, but scarcely a house in Broadstairs Road escaped some sort of damage, the thoroughfare being 'littered with glass, slates and tiles'. Several front doors were blown out. Subsequently this house was rebuilt and now exists as 30 Broadstairs Road. (*ITG*, 14 July 1944 and *Kelly's Isle of Thanet Directory for 1939*)

SECTION NINE

Education

HADDON DENE SCHOOL, BROADSTAIRS, 1933 advertisement, with small boys being received into an otherwise boarding- and day-school for girls, which had opened in 1929. (*ITG*, 7 October 1933)

HADDON DENE SCHOOL, 1950. Miss Vyse, with her pupils and teachers, celebrating the school's twenty-first birthday, boys being by now well in evidence. (*ITG*, 16 June 1950)

HOLY TRINITY VICARAGE LAWN, 1962. Girls from Haddon Dene School give a dancing display at the annual church fête. (*ITG*, 20 July 1962)

SALEM BAPTIST SCHOOLROOM, ST PETER'S, Thursday 31 March 1938. Mrs A. Rapson lays one of the foundation stones for an extension of the school, others being laid by Mrs M.A. Eveling and the Revd C.V. Evans. (*ITG*, 9 April 1938)

CHARLES DICKENS SCHOOL, BROADSTAIRS ROAD, on Wednesday 28 September 1955, an open day when parents were given the opportunity of viewing their children at work in the classrooms, in this case in the dressmaking class. This new school had been officially opened on Monday 12 September 1955 by Mr Philip Charles Dickens, grandson of the famous novelist, in the presence of 400 guests. (*ITG*, 30 September 1955)

WELLESLEY HOUSE SCHOOL, BROADSTAIRS, abutting on to Bromstone and Gladstone Roads, on Thursday 11 June 1957. Prince Richard, the present Duke of Gloucester, receives a kiss from his mother, the Duchess of Gloucester, now Princess Alice, on her arrival to attend a garden fête in aid of the Church of England Children's Society. Standing nearby are the chairman of the Broadstairs and St Peter's UDC, Cllr Mrs A.W. Mannell, the Mayor and Mayoress of Ramsgate, Alderman the Revd and Mrs Harcourt Samuel, the Marchioness of Linlithgow and the Archdeacon of Southwark, the Ven. H.H. Sands. On his right is Mrs Boyce, the wife of the headmaster, Mr J. Boyce MA. (*ITG*, 12 July 1957)

WELLESLEY HOUSE SCHOOL, Sunday 12 October 1969. The Duchess of Gloucester receives a bouquet of pink carnations from Charlotte Sale, the headmaster's five-year-old daughter, during a private visit to to open the newly merged Wellesley House and St Peter's Court preparatory schools. Pictured from right to left is Mr John Harris, head of the firm of architects responsible for the new building, Mr W.R. Rees-Davies MP, Charlotte's mother, Mrs C. Sale, and the late Mrs N.J. Sale, mother of the headmaster, Mr Bill Sale, who has recently retired after twenty-two years as headmaster of this exclusive Broadstairs preparatory school, which was established in 1900. The little boy seen clapping on the extreme left is John Gandolfo. (*TT*, 14 October 1969)

RIMPTON COURT BOYS' HOME, READING STREET, August 1955. A proud moment for the sports captain as he receives the Freddie Vass Cup from the donor, Mr F.L. Vass, his side having beaten visiting campers from Bow in a series of sports matches. Note in the background a paucity of residential development. (*ITG*, 26 August 1955)

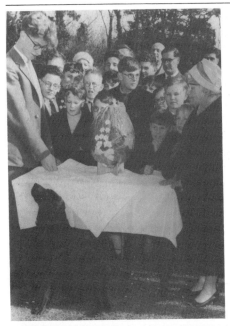

WHITENESS MANOR SCHOOL FOR CRIPPLED BOYS, KINGSGATE, Monday 27 March 1961, the wife of the chairman of the Broadstairs and St Peter's UDC, Mrs F.E.J. Amies, presenting a 'monster' Easter Egg to the head prefect, John Apps. The egg had been subscribed for by St Peter's residents through the good offices of confectioner, Mr G.E. Hallier of 7 Cecilia Grove. (*ITG*, 30 March 1961)

WHITENESS MANOR SCHOOL FOR CRIPPLED BOYS, Thursday 1 June 1961. Jack Warner, of *Dixon of Dock Green* fame, on arriving to open a garden fête, finds himself 'arrested' by three of the boys dressed as policemen. (*ITG*, 2 June 1961)

CALLIS COURT SCHOOL, ST PETER'S, 1959 Christmas party. (*ITG*, 24 December 1959)

HOLY TRINITY CHURCH OF ENGLAND BOYS' SCHOOL, Thursday 12 February 1970. Mr William Reed is pictured outside the school on his retirement as headmaster, following which the school was closed, the 115 pupils being transferred to the new Upton Primary School at Edge End Road, Broadstairs. (*ITG*, 13 February 1970)

THANET TECHNICAL COLLEGE, RAMSGATE ROAD, BROADSTAIRS, the School of Hotel Management and Catering Trades in April 1970. Three students taking a senior course in hotel management are pictured in the entrance lounge of the college 'hotel'. (*ITG*, 17 April 1970)

THANET TECHNICAL COLLEGE, April 1970. Mr Charles Wardman, lecturer in *haute cuisine*, is instructing students in the preparation of dishes to be served in the 'five star' restaurant. (*ITG*, 17 April 1970)

SECTION TEN

Sport

BROADSTAIRS REGATTA in 1894 with the four junior winners in the foreground. They were C. Wastall (stroke), P.H. Emerson (captain), J.W. Philipson, G. Fuggle (bow) and A.E. Stannard (cox). (*ITG*, 1 April 1939)

SAILING OFF BROADSTAIRS HARBOUR, late 1940s. Visible in the background are Eldon Place, Bleak House and Holy Trinity church. (Margate Museum)

BROADSTAIRS SAILING CLUB REGATTA, Sunday 27 July 1958. Over fifty boats were attracted from as far away as the Medway, Folkestone and Deal. (*ITG*, 1 August 1958)

GRAND BALLROOM, WEST CLIFF ROAD, BROADSTAIRS, Monday 16 October 1961. Fourteen of the twenty-four winners in the Broadstairs Sea Angling Festival pose for the camera after receiving their trophies, current attractions in the ballroom being publicised in the background. From left to right (with their numbered positions in brackets) are Mrs Ethel Lovett (1), Mr D. Holmes (2), Mr Jack M. Nye (3), the late Mr Ron Edwards (6), the late Mr A.F. McGavin (7), Miss C. Davis (8), the late Mr E.J. Bowyer (9), Mr Lew H. Bing (10), Mr Noel E. Winsley (13) and finally a half view of Mr V. Hawes (14). Mr Bing is holding the Broadstairs and St Peter's Sea Angling Society Challenge Cup for the greatest number of fish caught in any one day. (*ITG*, 20 October 1961)

BROADSTAIRS MEMORIAL RECREATION GROUND, late 1940s. A bowls match is in progress in front of the clubhouse of the Broadstairs and St Peter's Bowling Club, which was affiliated to the English Bowling and the Kent County Bowling Associations. According to the 1946 *Broadstairs Official Guide* this 'well-laid six-rink green [had] been kept in excellent condition throughout the war' and 'the members readily accord a hearty welcome to visitors and give opportunities for them to participate in their games during the morning, afternoon and evening sessions'. (Margate Museum)

BROADSTAIRS MEMORIAL RECREATION GROUND, Saturday 24 May 1952. Cllr A.T. Tucker, the chairman of the Broadstairs and St Peter's UDC, bowls one of the first woods at the official opening of the new bowling green, the adjacent hard tennis courts and the approach golf course. Behind him on his right is Mr Vernon Turner, president of the English Bowling Association, standing alongside Mr Harry Gilham, the secretary of the Broadstairs and St Peter's Bowling Club. (*ITG*, 30 May 1952)

MISS DIANA FISHWICK, daughter of Mr F.W. Fishwick of 'Durban', Reading Street, when she won the Girls' Open Golf Championship in 1927. In 1930 she went on to win the British Women's Open Golf Championship at Formby, following which, on her return to Broadstairs, the directors and managing committee of the North Foreland Golf Course entertained her to lunch. (*ITG*, 24 May 1930)

NORTH FORELAND GOLF COURSE, Sunday 16 August 1959. Critical spectators observe Bernard Hunt, one of four Ryder Cup golfers, getting himself out of bunker trouble in an exhibition match. (*ITG*, 21 August 1959)

ST PETER'S RECREATION GROUND, the grass tennis courts, late 1940s. (Margate Museum)

BROADSTAIRS MEMORIAL RECREATION GROUND, 1953. The new hard tennis courts are in use, with the railway and public footpath alongside. Note, compared to today, a paucity of buildings beyond the courts. (Margate Museum)

HILDERSHAM HOUSE, BROADSTAIRS, Friday 25 May 1956. Mr G.C.L. Baker leads the Broadstairs cricket team on to the field for a match against Kent. Facing a total of 211 runs, Broadstairs in an exciting finish reached 202 for nine wickets at the close of play. (*ITG*, 1 June 1956)

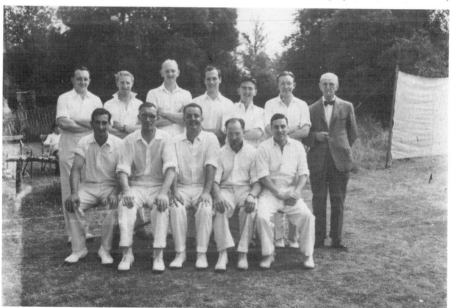

BROADSTAIRS CRICKET TEAM, 1957, 'one of the most prolific run-getting sides in Thanet'. From left to right, back row, are: P.E. Smith, R.D. Saunders, J. Wells, G. Burley, J.B. Savage, P.S. Holmes and F.E. Mann. Front row: R.J. Cohen, R.H. Jowsey, G.C.L. Baker (captain), L.P. Sampson and W. Anthony. (*ITG*, 12 July 1957)

CATHOLIC CHURCH OF OUR LADY STAR OF THE SEA, Edge End Road, Broadstairs on Saturday 10 February 1934, when members of the Broadstairs and District Rifle Club formed an archway of rifles at the marriage of Miss Mercy Mary Forde, eldest daughter of Cllr J.A. Forde JP, and Mrs Forde, of 'Templemore', St Peter's Road, Broadstairs to Mr Kenneth Ralph Gray, only son of Mr and Mrs R.F. Gray, of 'Greylands', Edgar Road, Margate. The church had been opened and dedicated on 10 September 1931 by the Rt Revd Peter E. Amigo, the Bishop of Southwark. (*ITG*, 17 February 1934)

BROADSTAIRS FOOTBALL CLUB, 1903/4 season. The club enjoyed a boom time this season and won the Thanet League championship. Members of the team are: William Harman, Jack Silk, James Blythman, Jack Pettit (goalkeeper), George Price, Billy Edwards, William Price, James Wraight, Charlie Culver, Billy Scott, Ronnie Stephens, Willie Smith, Albert 'Sooty' Olive (the skipper), the two Fenton brothers, W.F. Goodall, Bill Smith and Billy Marsh, pictured with the rector of Broadstairs, the Revd F.T. Mills. The club did not survive the Second World War. (*ITG*, 4 and 11 February 1955)

ST PETER'S RECREATION GROUND, Saturday 10 January 1970. A Dover forward is resolutely halted in his tracks by one of the Thanet Wanderers pack, the Wanderers winning this rugby match by thirty-three points to three. Grange Road is in the background. (*ITG*, 16 January 1970)

BROADSTAIRS PUTTING GREEN, VICTORIA PARADE, 1960s, with a family in earnest play. (Margate Museum)

THE ANNUAL BROADSTAIRS HORSE SHOW at St Peter's Recreation Ground, on Wednesday 3 August 1955, where children are making friends with one of the huntsman's horses. (*ITG*, 5 August 1955)

THE BROADSTAIRS HORSE SHOW at St Peter's Recreation Ground, August 1958. Some of the hundreds of spectators watch the show from the comfort of deck-chairs, with the houses of Norman Road behind the trees. (*ITG*, 8 August 1958)

SECTION ELEVEN

Entertainment

THE GARDEN-ON-THE-SANDS PAVILION, 1946, with Ken Frank's Broadstairs Revellers, on the steps behind a poster advertising their show. (Margate Museum)

THE PLAYHOUSE, WESTCLIFF AVENUE, October 1950, where the Broadstairs Dickens Fellowship's production of Bleak House played to large audiences. From left to right: Sheila Campbell, Harold Thornley, Myrtle Nuthall, Margaret Austin and Mollie Steward. Several repertory companies had successful runs at the Playhouse in its heyday. (*ITG*, 27 October 1950)

THE PAVILION, 1953. An evening concert with Cecil Barker and his orchestra. (Margate Museum)

THE BOHEMIA THEATRE in the High Street, mid-1950s. This circus act was among the shows presented by Jerry and Bobby Jerome. (Margate Museum)

THE BOHEMIA THEATRE, mid-1950s, with six chorus girls on stage. Prior to its becoming derelict and burning to the ground, concert parties in the Bohemia attracted full houses. (Margate Museum)

THE BOHEMIA THEATRE, 29–31 December 1954, showing the entire cast of Aladdin, the pantomime presented by the local Buffaloes Lodge, written and produced by Mr J.P. Huckstep of High Street, St Peter's. Len Taylor was the wicked Abanaza, Tom Fasham the pig-tailed He Sat, the part of Aladdin being played by Pat Howard. Note the pianist smoking a cigarette. What was an 'ambitious eight-scene pantomime' received a favourable press review. 'Panto had bright features', including 'scenery and costumes'. (*ITG*, 7 January 1955)

THE GRAND BALLROOM 1960s, with dancing to 'Al Clark and His Music'. (Margate Museum)

THE BANDSTAND, mid-1950s. The seated audience listens to an evening concert, Ted Farley performing at the organ; the kiosk is open for light refreshments. The bandstand has occupied its present site since 1952. (Margate Museum)

'TWO MUSICAL SPOTLIGHTS' AT THE BANDSTAND, 1961. Ted Farley, 'ace organist and entertainer' with Yvonne Mehro, his wife, 'a charming singer and hostess'. That year their 'Happy Family Show' involved music, singing, action songs, competitions and games. (Margate Museum)

THE BANDSTAND, C. 1949, with Bobby Pagan at the Compton organ. (Margate Museum)

THE BANDSTAND, 1952. The promenade lights are on in an attractive setting for outside old-time dancing to Sid Randall's orchestra. Otherwise Ted (E.J.) Farley provided musical performances on the Compton organ. (Margate Museum)

SECTION TWELVE

Royal Occasions

HIGH STREET, BROADSTAIRS. The 1926 visit to Thanet, on Wednesday 24 November, of HRH the Prince of Wales, the future King Edward VIII, included a journey in an open car from Ramsgate to Margate through Broadstairs, St Peter's and Kingsgate, attracting great crowds along the beautifully decorated route. Dressed in a grey overcoat and wearing a blue tie and a bowler hat, the prince is photographed sitting behind his chauffeur, Mr W.S. Castle. He is entering the High Street from the Victoria Parade near to Dickens House. Note the white posts which had been erected to prevent cars, etc. from trespassing on to the Promenade. (*ITG*, 27 November 1926)

SILVER JUBILEE CELEBRATIONS of their Majesties King George V and Queen Mary at St Peter's Recreation Ground, 1935, Cllr B.J. Pearson, the chairman of the Broadstairs and St Peter's UDC, addressing the assembled children. Immediately behind him is Cllr F. Foster and, to his right, Cllr E. Kirkham Minter. (*ITG*, 11 May 1935)

CORONATION DAY, Wednesday 12 May 1937, saw a happy group of boys at Broadstairs, some waving flags. (*ITG*, 15 May 1937)

HRH THE DUKE OF KENT visiting Thanet on Thursday 1 June 1939. Cllr F. Foster, the chairman of the Broadstairs and St Peter's UDC, enjoys a joke with the duke as they leave his car at Broadstairs. (*ITG*, 3 June 1939)

PIERREMONT HALL, 1 June 1939. The Duke of Kent admires the medals being proudly worn by old soldiers, one of whom is Mr George Bance, the caretaker of the council offices in Pierremont Hall. (*ITG*, 3 June 1939)

HRH THE DUKE OF KENT IN BROADSTAIRS, 1 June 1939. His Royal Highness showed a particular interest in the nursing and ambulance services of the British Red Cross Society at Broadstairs. Here he is seen inspecting the nurses, accompanied by the chairman of the Broadstairs and St Peter's UDC, Cllr F. Foster. (*ITG*, 3 June 1939)

FAIRFIELD HOUSE RESIDENTIAL SCHOOL, Saturday 16 September 1950. Eager children show the Countess Mountbatten of Burma around the grounds. The countess was president of the Save the Children fund, which owned the school. (*ITG*, 22 September 1950)

THE PAVILION, Saturday 9 June 1951. Battersea old folk welcome the Duchess of Gloucester, accompanied by Cllr A.T. Tucker, the chairman of the Broadstairs and St Peter's UDC and the Revd Thompson of the Battersea Central Mission, who was instrumental in bringing Battersea old folk to Broadstairs for short holidays. (*ITG*, 15 June 1951)

BANDSTAND AND CLOCK TOWER, 1950s, in front of an impressive firework display. (Margate Museum)

PIERREMONT HALL, floodlit and decorated for the 1953 coronation. (Margate Museum)

BANDSTAND AND CLOCK TOWER, floodlit for the 1953 coronation. (Margate Museum)

Special or Notable Events

ANNUAL CAROL CONCERT, 1969. A boar's head is presented to the concert's well-known conductor, the Rt Hon. Mr Edward Heath, standing in front of the chairman of the Broadstairs and St Peter's UDC, Cllr L. Rigelsford. (*TT*, 16 December 1969)

HOLY TRINITY CHURCH on Thursday 15 October 1936 was the scene for a sacred concert and recital given by an East End choir comprising the boys of St Mary of the Angels' Song School, in east London. (*ITG*, 17 October 1936).

BANDSTAND, VICTORIA GARDENS, C. 1950, fancy-dress competition, entries Nos 72 and 83; entry 72 being Colin Whyman, the author's brother, 'returning to school', wearing the uniform of the Chestnuts School, Rochester. (Mrs V.G. Whyman)

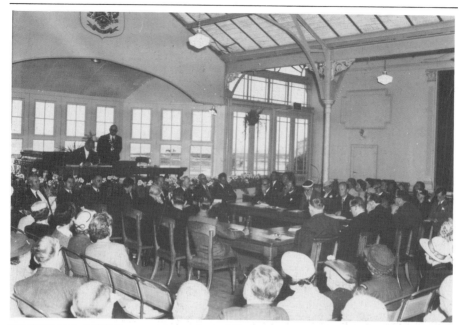

THE PAVILION. In 1956 the annual meeting of the Broadstairs and St Peter's UDC was held here for the first time, when Cllr H.E. Seccombe was elected chairman for the second consecutive year. (*ITG*, 25 May 1956)

THE ARCHBISHOP OF CANTERBURY, Dr Geoffrey Fisher, enjoys a joke with Cllr Mrs A.W. Mannell, the chairman of the Broadstairs and St Peter's UDC, at a civic dinner on Wednesday 30 October 1957. On the left are Cllr and Mrs H. Noble. (*ITG*, 1 November 1957)

THE MAIN BAY, Thursday 28 July 1949. A crowd estimated at 30,000 surged over the sands to greet 40 bearded Vikings who had rowed from Denmark to Broadstairs, commemorating the landing of Hengist and Horsa 1,500 years before. Waiting to greet them in Danish was Prince Georg, the Crown Prince of Denmark, wearing the uniform of a lieutenant of the Danish army. In this photograph 'a bathing belle prepares to "shoot" the "invaders" with her camera.' (*ITG*, 29 July 1949)

THE MAIN BAY, 28 July 1949: 'Some of the bearded Vikings'. Following this landing the Broadstairs and St Peter's UDC renamed the Main Bay as Viking Bay. (*ITG*, 29 July 1949)

VICTORIA GARDENS, Thursday 9 August 1956. Paul and Nigel Sutherland, Broadstairs twins, won the first prize at the Broadstairs water sports as Hengist and Horsa. (*ITG*, 10 August 1956)

BROADSTAIRS DICKENS FESTIVAL, 1964, being opened at the Garden-on-the-Sands Pavilion by the chairman of the Broadstairs and St Peter's UDC, Cllr E.V. Neville, with three-year-old Celia Peppiatt admiring his chain of office. (*TT*, 16 June 1964)

BROADSTAIRS DICKENS FESTIVAL, 1964. Festival-goers watch a Punch and Judy show in the grounds of the Albion Hotel, with onlookers. Suzanne's gift shop and Dickens House are in the background. Standing in front of Suzanne's, on the right, is Mrs P. Lowings and to her right is Miss P. Briggs. On the extreme left is Mrs W. Peppiatt. (*TT*, 16 June 1964)

BROADSTAIRS CARNIVAL PROCESSION, 1961. A colourful river-boat, mounted by the Broadway traders, is ready to be towed away by a tractor. (*ITG*, 18 August 1961)

VICTORIA PARADE, mid-1960s, with floats in the Broadstairs Carnival, the '18 Hole Putting Green' being prominently advertised. (Margate Museum)

BROADSTAIRS CARNIVAL PROCESSION, 1964, headed by the Central Band of the Women's Royal Air Force. (*TT*, 11 August 1964)

PIERREMONT PARK, August 1970, one of the traditional dances in the annual programme of the Broadstairs Folk Festival, then in its fifth year. (*ITG*, 14 August 1970)

Right:
BROADSTAIRS AND ST PETER'S 1944 Holiday Week. Jean Pearce, the sixteen-year-old schoolgirl daughter of W/O G.A.T. Pearce, RAF, and Mrs Pearce, of 18 Alexandra Road, was appointed 'Queen of the Week' by popular vote. (*ITG*, 11 August 1944)

Below:
'MISS BROADSTAIRS', 1949, Miss Maureen Gould, and to her left the film star, John Blythe. Note the intriguing heading. (*ITG*, 19 August 1949)

"MISS BROADSTAIRS"
BARRED BATHING DRESS

FILM STARS' POPULAR CHOICE

'MISS BROADSTAIRS', 1961, Denise Collins, with the Morelli Challenge Cup. (Margate Museum)

'WATER SPORTS QUEEN', 1959, Miss Yvonne Mackenzie from Greenock, Scotland, having her sash adjusted by Cllr E.F. Owen, the chairman of the Broadstairs and St Peter's UDC, in the Victoria Gardens. (*ITG*, 28 August 1959)

THE BANDSTAND, Saturday 21 June 1969. Broadstairs artists hang their work for a one-day exhibition. (*TT*, 24 June 1969)

PROMENADE OVERLOOKING VIKING BAY, 1958. Spectators observe the swimming races during the annual Broadstairs water sports and gala. (*ITG*, 22 August 1958)

BROADSTAIRS WATER GALA, 1965. The 'Crazy Cops' arrive by boat to break up the battle between the Millers and Sweeps in Broadstairs harbour, the beach and promenade being absolutely packed for this annual spectacle. (*ITG*, 20 August 1965)

BROADSTAIRS WATER GALA, 1968. In a new event, again being observed by a vast crowd, the victims of King Neptune's Court were lathered, shaved and made to walk the plank. (*ITG*, 23 August 1968)

VICTORIA GARDENS, 1969, the scene of the August Bank Holiday Seafront Fayre, held by Broadstairs Rotary Club. This tug-of-war contest was won by Fords of Dagenham, with the Broadstairs team, pictured, in second place. The Fayre raised £1,300 in aid of local causes. (*TT*, 3 September 1969)

BROADSTAIRS ROTARY CLUB CAROL TOUR, 1954, where Father Christmas collected gifts for children's homes. (*ITG*, 23 December 1954)

PARK HALL, PIERREMONT GARDENS, Friday 25 February 1955. In what was a snowy, severe winter there was a poor attendance at the Broadstairs and St Peter's Over Sixties Club monthly whist drive, but even so a few members turned up trumps! (*ITG*, 4 March 1955)

SECTION FOURTEEN

Famous Local Personalities

KINGSGATE CASTLE HOTEL, May 1937. 'Miss Australia', Miss Sheila Martin, is pictured with Lord Gifford, seated, Mr R.F. Pearce, the hotel's managing director, and Mr Huntley Wright. (*ITG*, 29 May 1937)

THE DEATH OF VISCOUNT NORTH-CLIFFE on Monday 14 August 1922. The founder of the *Daily Mail* was well-known in Thanet, having resided at Elmwood, St Peter's for many years, and being also an uncle of Thanet's MP, the Hon. Esmond Harmsworth. (*ITG*, 19 August 1922)

THE HON. ESMOND C. HARMSWORTH MP, the only surviving son of Lord Rothermere, was the Conservative candidate in the 1922 general election, defending a majority of 2,653 which he more than doubled to 5,890. (*ITG*, 5 February 1921)

MR W.R. REES-DAVIES, Conservative MP for Thanet, on Thursday 26 May 1955, asking children at Rumfields, St Peter's, 'Has your mother voted?' In the general election held on that day he retained his seat with a comfortable majority of 12,289. (*ITG*, 27 May 1955)

THE PAVILION, Saturday 21 November 1959. Mrs W.R. Rees-Davies, wife of the Conservative MP for Thanet, having opened the Conservative Fête, tried her luck on the roll-a-penny stall. On her right is Mr S.R. Gay, the chairman of the local Conservative Association. (*ITG*, 27 November 1959)

THE RT HON. MR EDWARD HEATH MP, having attended the Palm Sunday service in St Peter's church in 1966, signing autographs after leaving the church. (*TT*, 5 April 1966)

THE RT HON. MR EDWARD HEATH, guest of honour at the Conservative Diners' club, studying the menu at the Clarendon Hotel on Thursday 29 December 1966, with Mr W.R. Rees-Davies, MP for Thanet, and Cllr Edward Robinson, the chairman of the Broadstairs and St Peter's UDC, on the right. (*TT*, 3 January 1967)

MR W. WALSH, of Westover Road, St Peter's, August 1936, England's oldest tram driver, still fit at seventy-eight and with 350,000 miles in Thanet to his credit, about to board his favourite tram, No. 44. Contrary to his hopes, the Thanet tram services were discontinued during March 1937. (*ITG*, 22 August 1936)

DOWN YOUR WAY IN BROADSTAIRS. The principal of the YMCA College, Kingsgate, Mr Clifton Robbins, is interviewed by Franklin Engelman for the BBC Light Programme on Sunday 12 August 1956. (*ITG*, 10 August 1956)

THE LANCASTER HOTEL, Saturday 21 February 1970, showing members and guests at the annual dinner of the Broadstairs and St Peter's Labour Party, with guest speaker, Mr Ron Hayward. (*ITG*, 27 February 1970)

PIERREMONT HALL, Wednesday 24 June 1964. Over thirty librarians from all parts of Kent attended a meeting of the Kent Division of the Association of Assistant Librarians. From left to right are: Cllr E.V. Neville, chairman of the Broadstairs and St Peter's UDC, Mr R. Atkins, chairman of the Kent division, Mr John Hoyle, National President of the Association and Deputy Librarian at Oldham, and Mr John Walters, Broadstairs librarian. (*TT*, 30 June 1964)

ST ANDREW'S CHURCH, READING STREET, Tuesday 13 April 1961. The Bishop of Dover, the Rt Revd L.E. Meredith, is seen talking to Mr H.M. Steed JP, a churchwarden, after the fiftieth anniversary service, with the vicar of St Peter's, the Revd T.E. Prichard, on the left. The bishop preached to a congregation of about 250 people, following which refreshments were served in the church hall. (*ITG*, 14 April 1961)

HOLY TRINITY CHURCH, Wednesday 14 June 1961. The rector, the Revd Basil Gibbs, admires a twenty-three-inch television set presented to him by his parishioners to mark his twenty-five years in holy orders. Also in the picture, from left to right, are: Miss F.J. Woods, church council secretary, Mr J. Hardiman, the rector's warden, and Mr W.J. Reed, the people's warden. (*ITG*, 16 June 1961)

REVD T. PRICHARD, the vicar of St Peter's, in October 1957, standing alongside a new Morris Minor, WKM 898, funded and presented by grateful parishioners, with Mrs Prichard acting as chauffeur. (*ITG*, 11 October 1957)

CANON T. PRICHARD, Tuesday 16 April 1968, being presented with a cheque from the parishioners of St Peter's by Mr R. Stockwell, churchwarden, at a farewell reception, with Mrs Prichard looking on. After nearly fifteen years as vicar of St Peter's he moved on to become Archdeacon of Maidstone and a residentiary canon of Canterbury cathedral. (*ITG*, 19 April 1968)

THE ARCHBISHOP OF CANTERBURY, the Most Revd Dr Michael Ramsey, and the new vicar of St Peter's, the Revd John Haviland Russel de Sausmarez, in conversation as they walked into St Peter's church before the service of institution and induction on Friday 24 May 1968. (*ITG*, 31 May 1968)

BROADSTAIRS CONGREGATIONAL CHURCH, YORK STREET, on Wednesday 1 September 1965, was filled to overflowing for the induction of the Revd Kenneth Thomas Walters. Standing outside and in front of the notices advertising services and the induction are, from left to right: the president of the Ramsgate and Broadstairs Free Church Council, the Revd T.J. Lewis, the Revd H.W. Gurney, the Moderator of the Southern Province, the Revd W. Andrew James, the Revd Kenneth Walters, the chairman of the Broadstairs and St Peter's UDC, Cllr E.V.L. Neville, the Revd W.R. Stokes, and Mr T.A. Peters. (*ITG*, 3 September 1965)

MISS GLADYS WATERER, organizer of the Broadstairs Dickens Festival for thirty years, meeting eight-year-old Clare Gilham, appearing in Miss Waterer's 1967 adaptation of *Pickwick*. (*TT*, 20 June 1967)

MR LES BEAK, the Broadstairs Entertainments and Publicity Manager, at the Pavilion, 1964. (*TT*, 18 August 1964)

MR FRED WARD, Pierremont Hall, March 1971. The clerk to the Broadstairs and St Peter's UDC, Mr K. Denne, presents stereo equipment to his deputy, Mr Fred Ward, on his retirement after thirty-five years in local government in Broadstairs. Because of his unrivalled knowledge of local affairs, he earned the title, 'Mr Broadstairs'. (*TT*, 30 March 1971)

ACKNOWLEDGEMENTS

I am particularly grateful to Mr M. Pearce, the editor, and members of the editorial staff for permitted access to and the reproduction of photographs which have appeared in the *Isle of Thanet Gazette* and the *Thanet Times*; likewise, to Mr C. Wilson MBE, BEM, the Museum Curator of Margate Museum for permission to borrow and select over many months the Broadstairs Sunbeam photographs, which form part of the museum's photographic archive. I am scarcely less indebted to Mr J.T.R. Styles, photographer at the University of Kent, and to his assistant, Mr J. West, for drawing my attention to some Victorian photographs of Broadstairs and for reproducing the original Sunbeam photographs. Without their kind assistance the production of this book would not have been possible. I am also grateful to Mr G.W. Everest for permission to reproduce his photograph of Broadstairs High Street as it appeared during the August Bank Holiday of 1940, and to Mrs V.G. Whyman for permission to reproduce three personal photographs in her possession.

The following have been very kind in allowing me to visit them and, in some cases, for giving up considerable amounts of their time in providing advice and information which have proved crucial in terms of dating and personal and other identification:

Mr and Mrs T.N. Attwell • Mr L.C. Beak • Mr Lew W. Bing • Mr J. Bowyer
Mr A.W. Bridges • Mrs N. Bridges • Mr S. Clark
Mrs Y. Farley • Mr G.L. Foord • Mr H. Goode • Mr A.J. Pay • Mr B. Sale
Miss J. Smith • Mr G.A. Strevens • Mr and Mrs F.H. Ward.

Final thanks are also due to Mrs E. Stoydin, my secretary in the university, for showing considerable patience in typing and retyping the manuscript and to my mother, Mrs V.G. Whyman, for having assisted me with proof-reading and transport.